PRAISE FOR MARJORIE J. LEVINE'S POETRY

"This verse is indeed a beautiful and comprehensive road trip through time and recollection. The repeated word selection and language style intimately acquaints us with the author and allows us to experience her symbolism and missed opportunities as our own. The line between real and imagined is perfectly blurred, inviting us to travel back and forth in the writer's life while knocking gently at the door of our own memories."

~Nicole Freezer Rubens, author
The Long Pause and the Short Breath

"Absolutely beautiful! Makes any comment I could say about this poem hereafter, seem superficial. I love the imagery. Left me on the verge of tears."

~Reader comment posted for
WHAT WAY TO GO TODAY, *The Daily Beat* blog

"After diving deeper into (CODA), I find it all the more beautiful and heart wrenching. Lovely work."

~Charly Santagado, *Pinky Thinker Press*

D0872968

ROAD TRIPS
poems

Marjorie J. Levine

The Three Tomatoes Book Publishing

Copyright © 2021 by Marjorie J. Levine

All rights reserved. No part of this book may be reproduced in any form or by any electronic or mechanical means including information storage and retrieval systems, without permission in writing from the publisher. The only exception is by a reviewer, who may quote short excerpts in a review. For permission requests, please address The Three Tomatoes Publishing.

Published June 2021

ISBN: 978-1-7364949-3-6
Library of Congress Cataloging-in-Publication Data

For information address:
The Three Tomatoes Book Publishing
6 Soundview Rd.
Glen Cove, NY 11542

Cover, interior and back photos courtesy of Marjorie J. Levine

Cover and interior design: Susan Herbst

All company and/or product names may be trade names, logos, trademarks, and/or registered trademarks and are the property of their respective owners.

for Maurice

CONTENTS

NAP TIME
WHAT WAY TO GO TODAY   3
NAP TIME   5
DAWN ON SEVENTH AVENUE   6
TWO DAYS TAKE ONE   7
SPINSTERS AND GHOSTS   8
OBSESSIVE-COMPULSIVE DISORDER   9
THE BOARDER   10
SWEATING MADNESS   11
MURMURS IN THE DARKNESS   12
THE WAY I LIVE   13
TWO DAYS   14
KIDDIE RIDES   15

DELINEATIONS
STREET LIGHTS   19
PALIMPSESTS IN THE HOUSE   21
ON 82ND STREET   23
BLOOD RUMINATIONS   26
CONNECTIONS IN THE LYRIC THEATER   27
THE SHILL   28
NOBODY IS HOME   29
BREAKING BREAD WITH A STRANGER   31
THE DISTANT LEFTOVER   32
INVOLUNTARY PASSAGES   33
THE STATION AND THE BAR   34
VINTAGE AIR   36
BORDENTOWN   38
REVISITED   40
DIFFERENT DROPS   43
BENDING TO ENTELECHY   45
THE EMPTY PARK   47
EYE PRINT MUSINGS   48
WHAT GROUNDS A TOWN   50
WHEREVER HE WAS TAKING ME   52

FISHNET STOCKINGS ON A COLD WINTER DAY   54
TUMBLEWEED   55
CHALKBOARD   56
DELINEATIONS   57
TRIPTYCH   58
SHIPWRECKED   59
THE WAY HE LOOKED AT HER   60
THE FLUID WALK   61
MANHATTAN BRIDGE THREE CENT LINE   62
SPILLED MILK   63
ALONE IN THE STILL   64
PLACE KALEIDOSCOPE   65
CODA   67
UNFINISHED WORK   68

SIX POEMS
OLD THINGS   71
IN THE PARK   72
PENTIMENTO   73
DEFINED SPACES   74
SENIORS   75
SLOWING DOWN   76

STREET POEMS
THIS PENTIMENTO   79
OPTICAL ILLUSION   80
PICTURE PERFECT   81
TO GET TO THIS PLACE   82
NOBODY HOME   83
MELANCHOLY   84
DESERTED HOUSES   85
WHERE THE ROAD STOPS   86

ACKNOWLEDGMENTS   91

ABOUT THE POET   93

NAP TIME

WHAT WAY TO GO TODAY

Almost dusk:
Last summer on one Wednesday, in July,
I sat on a bench, a grey wooden tired
Bench on a boardwalk out at old Long Beach.
In the sky a lonely and lost grey kittiwake tipped
As the hot pink sun set in blazing Technicolor over
Hot pinkish sand and the fading blue ocean water.

That morning:
I had thought about seeing great art...
Vermeer, or Courbet, or maybe Monet.
But, I drove to the beach instead to think
To think about everything creative that had been
Created before I got here, and when I was here,
And what will be created when I leave this place.
When one day I leave my place and all places in my
Consciousness that is now in this time and was
At a past time and will be in some next time;
Maybe all time exists at the same time.
The great minds of theoretical physicists search
For the "Theory of Everything" as they sit
In their cluttered rooms, their great thinking rooms.
In universities, they ponder the mathematical equations
And Schrödinger's cat and all those mysteries.

In the evening:
It is during the quiet and still and sad night when
I miss most the people I never met:
Edie Beale, and the Rat Pack, and even Rod Serling
Who made me want to time travel:
To go back to simpler places
Like Nedick's, or the Belmore, or Bickford's,
And Willoughby.
Then the longing, a longing when distant sounds
And faraway foghorns drive thoughts to reflect
On a life visible through some smoky cracked mirror,

A haunted and haunting steamy mirror.
As I am sort of old now and getting older
There is a vague and odd feeling that I,
Like the kittiwake, somehow must have lost the way.

NAP TIME

At dusk, a dream through stained glass:
In a hazy deciduous forest, I am almost naked—
Pristine gown clinging like translucent second skin,
Chartreuse satin slippers, cheeks pale porcelain rose,
And humidity turning my hair burnt sienna.
The scent of dried lavender drifts through trees—
"Alone in nature, by nature," ventriloquists murmur.
Bejeweled spiders, resting
On carefully crocheted cobwebs,
Melancholy widows, eyes green tourmaline,
A soldier seduced by indifference...
Haunted beauty washed forever in soft pink light.

A fading fragrant French cologne-
Earlier a sweet intoxicating elixir- melting and melted.
An elusive black-throated warbler,
Pausing on a great oak, bears witness:
An icon is shedding mellifluous silver tears,
Reflecting my grandfather, wrapped in his *tallit*
Stirring, turning, saying, "You look very familiar to me."

A clammy breeze passes through Manhattan.
I awaken this time, awakened last time,
Acquiescent and still, not knowing
If it is evening... or morning.

DAWN ON SEVENTH AVENUE

There is a moment of quiet stillness
Right before sunrise, before light;
When a clammy breeze passes
Through Manhattan
And nothing moves, nothing stirs.
My pristine gown clings in the humidity
Like translucent second skin.
I awaken, not knowing if it is evening…
Or morning.
See my reflection
In the haze of this smoky cracked mirror:
This is all I have ever been,
And all I will never be.

TWO DAYS TAKE ONE

One hot sunny Sunday, in July, at Long Beach
An amnesiac sat on the boardwalk watching
A strolling lady who was carrying a pearl-handled parasol.
A handsome soldier passed holding a love letter that was
Written on a faded lace white doily and a lonely spinster
Stared at vague images in the sand...
Lines soon to be scattered by an insouciant breeze.
An innocent, guileless, sienna-haired child
Paddled to shore in a teacup.
This is what happened on a hazy sunless Sunday,
In mid-August, at Westhampton.
A spiritual man, who once posed as an amnesiac,
Conducted past life regression sessions
In an old chartreuse theater and
A tattooed director, with wild cinematic aspirations,
Filmed the event in shades of mysterious grey.
Later, I rested on sands
And watched one lost kittiwake fly
In circles overhead while an organ played
Music from an invisible carousel.
I listened to the ocean and
Imagined mermaids swimming painlessly
In peaceful and seductive warm waters.
A sienna-haired child
Stepped out of a floating teacup,
And walked with sea legs
Along colorless sands.

SPINSTERS AND GHOSTS

It is murky and dim down the street
Where an unforgiving lonely spinster
Lives almost protected under blankets
Of carefully crocheted elixirs.

Here- where the ghosts of ancestors,
Sitting on the moss of invisible oaks,
Offer kind words of encouragement
Adding seconds to midnight
When dreams turn to film noir.

There- where starry-eyed children
With handsome fathers
Would spin until dusk... or dawn
On a forgotten Ferris wheel
Left behind by the carnival
After roadsters skidded home along
Slippery highways.

Now- up on a vacant fifth floor
The weariest is carefully coiffed and rouged,
Sitting on the other side of gold brocade.
Bloodless thighs wrapped in an opaque afghan,
She is clinging to a teacup of cold chamomile.

Later, she shares ambrosia with gods.
Then in a final gesture,
She scrapes and scrapes the bottom of her dish
Searching for one last drop.

OBSESSIVE-COMPULSIVE DISORDER

I catch a subtle whiff of dried lavender
As the director, a wiry-haired widow,
Lights a cigarette and with a simple single
Gesture flicks the ashes into the palm of her
Fashionably tattooed and manicured left hand.

"There is no need to state your full name;
Just speak of the fear, the constant fear,"
The director coaches.
Behind us, the steady swing and flutter of
Gold diaphanous curtains as a clammy, familiar breeze
Passes through the old chartreuse theater.

We describe strange, tormenting, ritualistic behavior:
Washing, checking, hoarding... mental anguish so
Exquisite the weariest sheds mellifluous tears:
"I've shared ambrosia with gods;
At midnight, demons turn my terror to film noir."

That evening, I dream of solitude
And the transmigration of souls...
One lonely soul wishing to return
Washed in amnesia, hypnotized and untainted.

When I awaken, it is still dark-
Down below, the street is eternally bathed
In disconsolate orange moonlight...
Trapped in an endless maze of mirrors.

THE BOARDER

Long ago...
A child rested on a maroon sofa
In the still musty living room
Of her grandmother's house.
The house was decorated with gold tassels
And white lace and starched doilies...
And it trapped a scent of burnt potato pancakes.
At night, the ghosts of ancestors sucked the juice
From the peaches of a backyard tree.

A fake fireplace electrically glowed
Orange-yellowish and whispered in
All seasons the child was home.
On a maroon table, sat an
Incandescent pink seashell...
"Hold it to your ear and you can hear
The sounds of the ocean," ventriloquists urged.

The steady whir and flutter of the slats
Of off-white Venetian blinds lulled her
As chill winds passed through Brooklyn.

At dusk, the front door opened and
A man, wearing grey and grey,
Silently traipsed through the house
To "his room" and he closed "his door."
He was home, too.

The grandmother called the man
Just "the boarder."
The child only glanced up as he passed and
He never spoke to her... nor she to him.

On the clearest of days she cannot even recall
His face... yet she stares at him whenever chill
Winds pass through Manhattan.

SWEATING MADNESS

Speak to me in hushed tones
And tell me who stole the peaches
From the old backyard tree
The night I danced the fandango
In front of a closed automat.
As the humidity of that evening
Turned my hair a burnt sienna
An elastic lady teased, "Tsk tsk,"
Because the chartreuse slippers I wore
Were not even my own.

Siamese twins took turns
Stroking the belly of an insect
That rested on the sterling silver tray
I held in my outstretched left hand.
A fading fragrant French cologne-
Earlier a sweet elixir-
Melted under the neon lights
At the very moment
The tattooed film director
Held a lit match to her cigarette
And started a small fire.

And the charlatan I once loved
Did a few fancy smart steps and knew,
As usual, I would forget.

MURMURS IN THE DARKNESS

She is not the first tenant who weeps
Into that stained pillow at night.

She limps to the window
And peeks out to face the pale moon
Jumping from one side to the other
While the heat of the evening
Becomes even more oppressive.

So! That bright star is not a star, after all!
"It is Jupiter," she murmurs.
The strange sound of a foghorn,
In the clear night, seems to place
Her in one moment and then another.

She tries to remember what
Passed from there to here,
From one time to this time...
But she is lost now like a
Prisoner in this nightmare,
This fantasy...

This fantasy or nightmare
In a thick veil of darkness.

THE WAY I LIVE

My memories have always been vague—
Arriving at dawn on Seventh Avenue
Or at the beach on a sunny hot Sunday,
Visible as peculiar visions in colorless sands.

In an old chartreuse theater, a wiry-haired
Director captured a slight shadowy piece
In muted shades of grey and grey.
But, I danced the wild fandango
In front of a closed automat
To try to forget.

Then one day I remembered
Everything, just like that...
Just as smooth as slipping into
Second skin.

But whether I remember
Or choose to forget,

The forgotten has always determined
The way in which I have lived.

TWO DAYS

One hot sunny Sunday, in July, at Long Beach:
An amnesiac sat on the boardwalk watching
A strolling lady who was carrying a pearl-handled parasol.
A handsome soldier passed holding a love letter that was
Written on a faded lace white doily and a lonely spinster
Stared at vague images in the sand...
Lines soon to be scattered by an insouciant breeze.

An innocent, guileless, sienna-haired child
Paddled to shore in a teacup.

This is what happened on a hazy sunless Sunday,
In mid-August, at Westhampton.
A spiritual man, who once posed as an amnesiac,
Conducted past life regression sessions
In an old chartreuse theater and
A tattooed director, with wild cinematic aspirations,
Filmed the event in shades of mysterious grey.

Later, I rested on sands
And watched one lost kittiwake fly
In circles overhead while an organ played
Music from an invisible carousel.

I listened to the ocean and
Imagined mermaids swimming painlessly
In peaceful and seductive warm waters.

A sienna-haired child
Stepped out of a floating teacup,
And walked with sea legs
Along colorless sands.
Sometimes before twilight,
I think of those two days.

Cut.

KIDDIE RIDES

I awakened and longed with desperation
To return to Brooklyn.
I wanted to ride until dawn on a creaky
Ferris wheel left behind by a carnival and
To visit the still standing luminous
Chartreuse home of my grandmother.
Memories behind stained glass windows
Beckoned like some naked amnesiac
Who struggles to reach home.

In the air, I could still smell the full bodied scent
Of burnt potato pancakes that wafted through that
House and I often glimpsed the ghosts of ancestors
Lurking and sucking juice from the backyard peach tree.
I longed with desperation to return to old Brooklyn.

At 5 P.M. I slipped into my car
And drove south through Manhattan.
The pink sun soon sizzled on the Hudson River
And set, to my right, in bright blazing Technicolor.
In the distance, one kittiwake
Seemed to have found the way.

I headed for the elixir of the spinning
Teacups: the kiddie rides at intoxicating
Coney Island... in the most haunted and
Haunting of places: Brooklyn.

DELINEATIONS

STREET LIGHTS

I bend to the streetlights as I am seduced by nostalgia:
Those heady elixirs that long ago were lit by candles
By strangers whose names sisters did not even know.
My knee touches old bricks where horse drawn carriages
Once waited to take families away to other places:
Familiar places or different places or any place.

On cloudy afternoons, lonely mothers stood in backyards
And hung the clean wash out to dry.
Children chased through the huge sheets that
Billowed and fell and almost touched the ground.
The frog in the grass bore witness.
The doll on the patch of colorless sand grew weaker.

At dusk, the dim streetlights reminded children to go inside
To leave the toys and the fading pale grey sky and the
Coming darkness that whispered it soon might rain.

At night, sad mothers knitted the same yellow sweaters
As they sat on the struggling sofas that filled the
Recesses of the window as the sudden yellow from the
Streetlights encouraged their gnarled fingers to keep
Going and going.

In mornings, I longed for my reflection through last night's
Stained glass: a prism that turned white light
To a kaleidoscope of colors
And pushed me to wherever.
But the streetlights of the previous night faded and
Turned my waking to film noir.

On a new dusk, the streetlamps went on and
Fathers returned home spent from war.
The director yelled "cut" and
The celluloid was seared
Into the ages.

In later years, I saw a bright marquee as I was walking down
The Great White Way and I wanted
To go the other way: to return to a simpler time
When nothing mattered except one light: a
Streetlight, that remained to always guide
The way home.

PALIMPSESTS IN THE HOUSE

Oh, you came to whisper and soothe me
Like a pale imposter and familiar burglar.
I was rendered weary and provoked to cover my ears
To hear nothing but the symphony of the mourning dove
Or children playing across the back yard
As they waited to grow.

All of the lofty promises in that same soft voice
Dripping with platitudes like the water from
The rain under the overpass
At the highway that takes so many away from here.

You with your fake standing ovations and
Confusing curtain calls.
I should have outsmarted you because I saw the clear signs.
You left eye prints in the dark as you peeked into
My dusty windows and your boots
Carved constant icy cold footprints
In the frozen snow outside my door.
Your chest was transparent.
Your heart was plastic.

I fell to my tattooed young knees believing you cared,
I went away and I came home to the same home.
My consciousness exploded into a disparity
Where all time exists at the same time.
So when you tried to feed me
I searched for a breast.
When you tried to seduce me
I closed my eyes and childishly pretended
I was asleep.

As I aged, I accepted the crumbs
From indifferent strangers
And when I was alone

I begged intruders to care about me.
Within all of my road trips you were like a
Thief who stole my wail.
When I finally left one autumn morning
There was nothing left:
Not the dry songs we sang or the memory of the day
We danced the tango in front of that closed automat.

I was saved by a signpost: DETOUR
When I stopped at a service station and was served.
I dined on a savory meal that when digested
Dissolved you into
Not even a tattered rumination.

ON 82ND STREET

Diary entry in the late afternoon:
The grey clouds above cling together
Trying hard not to let thin patches of blue
Peek through because the view might be less
Mysterious and other smoky clouds are so low
That they touch the patches of green grass and
The damaged dirt and set the graphics into stone
As all sad echoes fall away.

On this street, the boarded up windows of
The third house give me reasons to cry.

The side window that sat behind a steady
Whir and flutter of old Venetian blinds sits
Naked now displaying no eye prints.

The back window that once had chiffon frilly curtains
That fell out of that open window and even swayed
In the still night air, the window through which
I heard the constant flow of traffic
As roadsters skidded home on the
Slippery wet highway... is boarded up too.

The front window, where I sat with a caring and
Kind grandma who bought me a black velvet
Party dress and promised me a bride doll and took me to
A crowded playground with seesaws and gave me
A chocolate ice cream bar with sprinkles that are
Still melting in my mouth... is all opaque and dark.

The scent of my mother's heady aldehydic perfume must
Still haunt the narrow halls of the old house where
The dust and ashes of the tall plant I watered must still
Lay scattered on the basement floor.
I suppose the fake fireplace, that radiated electric light on a

Black and white old room that was filled with
Mahogany furniture and had closets that
Smelled of mothballs which were filled
With Zoot suits, is gone too.
And a kitchen that had a stove with
Pans of burnt potato pancakes has
Chartreuse wallpaper that is now a peculiar pentimento.
The succulent and ripe peaches from that old backyard tree
Have disappeared. I can still hear some old man across the
Alley calling for his cigar while his wife
Had drinks with her lover in a fancy gazebo.

There is the memory of the mirthful guy in a secret room
At the top of the stairs who, after I burst in, stood
Covering his private parts with a pair of boxers.
He showed me pictures once of the time he was a soldier
During WWII when he was stationed in the
Aleutian Islands and I did a double take.
He was posing with Virginia Mayo and
There were indifferent outtakes resting on the snow.

The bathroom, that once smelled of patchouli and
Always had a fresh bar of hot pink soap
Except in winter when the soap was
Lime green, had small soaps
Shaped like yellow ducks too.

Written at dusk:
I was jolted into the now when the startling sound of
Music suddenly filled the air.
What cinema music director was looking out of his
Own window on that street and turned up
Tchaikovsky's *Symphony No. 5, II* to
Provide the soundtrack to this disconsolate experience?

The strong bench in front of the first house that faced
The avenue where two couples sat to enjoy a spring day
Is rusty now and covered in mold and flies.

What a monster aging is.
Life kindly allows us little stays of execution along the way
Until the Grim Reaper inevitably
Sentences us all to the same horrifying data wipe:
Clear history and catch amnesia.

At 11:59 PM:
But until that day, on this day that I went back to
82nd Street, I knew the day was not my last day...
And I was glad that on 82nd Street
I could remember.

BLOOD RUMINATIONS

This tapestry is smeared with the
Blood of past ruminations
And failures.

Yet, it is nothing special
Or remarkable or outstanding.
It whispers of insignificance.
The trapeze artist slips
The dog walker drops the lead
And the baker spills the sugar.

Slow down,
There's a fork in the road:
Go the other way, things can change.
Undo the tangled mess created by
Uninvited trespassers
Who in your unguarded moments stole
The songs from your personal jukebox
And played them when you were not watching
And made them their own.
Cry for who you could have been
And go paint in blended watercolors a new picture.
Make it shine and make it drip
Like the sweet candy that you rolled around
On your tongue on hot summer days
When you were young and nobody was looking.
Taste that candy still in your mouth:
You never really digested it
It's still there, set like a frozen sculpture
That visitors in museums come to view
When they gawk at fine art.

CONNECTIONS IN THE LYRIC THEATER

The indifferent early night mist slides in from the
Hudson River and passes over four still avenues
Until it hits a main avenue and then it rests.

The ballerina stops spinning
The musician drops his violin
And the old man pays a quarter to see a peep show.

Later, he threw his ticket
On the wet pavement where it was carried to the curb
And all parts of him from the minutes were taken away.
He had no more reasons to go home.
So he climbed to the balcony of the
Lyric Theater and he sat too close to us
To intrude, to peek, or to steal glimpses.

And when I bit into yellow button candy
My mouth filled with sweet succulence
And watered, so you sucked the juice off my lips
Because you were thirsty.
Your tongue turned yellow like the egg
My sister painted the day before Easter.

And the old man left the theater.
Later, the old man rode a ferry to a penny arcade
And paid another quarter so a wooden fortune teller
Who sat inside a glass booth could pump out
A card with a prediction of his future.
"Go the other way, go a different way
To be taken far away so your days
Are no longer blurred."

The old man dropped the card into the water
As he rode the same ferry home.
And years later when he was even older
The evening he saw the peep show seemed
Almost hallucinogenic.

THE SHILL

Do you remember the night I told you the charlatan
Stroked the bellies of two insects that the jester placed on
A gold tray that he held in his outstretched left hand?

Do you recall the lonely spinster who
Lived almost protected under blankets
Of carefully crocheted elixirs?

Or how about the magnificent blue haired lady who was
Walking under a pearl-handled parasol in the
Hot summer evening when a handsome soldier passed
Holding a love letter that was written in Esperanto
On a faded lace white doily?

Forgive my machinations.
It was just an intermission.

The gnome guarded my precious jewels and treasures
The elastic lady gifted me with her flexibility and pearls
And the strongman slept on a bed of nails
That hid his tinctures.

And then they all gathered as a zephyr pulled my secrets out
Of a hat and I felt exposed, my skeletons no longer shielded.

The magician who I loved told me he was
Victor Mature and in the sharp light of morning,
After the circus left town, I realized
He lied too.
So I shed mellifluous silver tears
And returned to my own tent under the stars
And performed in my own after show.

NOBODY IS HOME

On a rainy chilly Monday night, I kneeled
On a broken rocky sidewalk where
Flawed vintage Halloween masks
Were buried under sticky patches of mud.
Yesterday's chipped and discarded
Dolls, dressed in wet petticoats,
Were still waiting to be adopted and taken
To new homes.

In the morning, the muted sun rose on the right
Over the bay and over the fading streetlights and the
Fragile bridge and the frail blue highway.
The hospital, now decorated for Christmas, is
Where babies are born: on the other side of the
Water and the place where soldiers still go to die.

Weep for the grey bent park with the broken rickety
Seesaw next to poor swings that from decades ago are
Still moving and the ice cream bar that once was frozen
Is still frozen under the empty barren jungle gym.

Bear witness to a pentimenti:
Night dives on a sliding pond,
Dips in a swimming pool or spins
On a Flying Horses Carousel with
Painted colorful ponies for young visitors
To ride and a bench where mothers sat as
They all went around and around and around
And no child ever grabbed the brass ring.

On the green grass, you chased little frogs that once swam in
A stream when they were tadpoles... and on cold nights
I slept in the small clear bedroom with a carved image of
Pinocchio on the wall during an evening the ice from my
Father's shoes dripped on the green worn carpet when he
Returned home from his lover's home.

Now what remains is the same highway lit only after dark
And the sound of the old cars as they still struggle to
Reach their own homes.

BREAKING BREAD WITH A STRANGER

During large gatherings,
I always dined alone in my room
And savored the meal.

There were no distractions:
No loud arguments
No political debates
No family photos to view
And no fake smiles or phony laughs through
Which to suffer.

There was no vacuous noise in my left ear.
The uncles worried about Aunt Ruth, who was
Taking a break from Bingo, every cousin thinking
She might fall asleep at the wheel.

Those were the days when at midnight
I would rest on the patio hammock
And look up at the night sky and imagine
The holiday dinners that would roll out into my future.

Decades later, on a snowy Sunday,
I walked to Bickford's and sat at the counter
All alone in the back.
My company was an old book
I picked up at the Strand:
The Secret of the Old Clock.

There was unexpected solace in
The visual rerun.
A man sat down near to me
And he soon dined on beef stew.
He looked weary and he carried
On his shoulders the weight of stone blocks.
I moved closer to him
As if the closeness would attach me to
An unfamiliar comfort: A sweet zone that was
Strange yet oddly made me feel secure.

THE DISTANT LEFTOVER

You with your constant smell of indifference
And I so hungry for even a sweet side glance.

But it was not to happen.
Maybe it was fate on the snowy evening I sailed
Away from you:
The last night I entered that ferry
The same ferry that always took me back to you
Because I was seduced by silly things
That never mattered.

I must have looked so crumbled, so forlorn,
That a nun stopped reading the Bible and moved
To sit closer to me, to give me comfort
And solace… and she did.

As I drifted the waters to reach my home
You disappeared and grew smaller in every way
Possible, so in many of my later years you
Became a blurred washed memory.

And after a great time, when my forgotten passion
Surfaced and took hold of me,
When the longing that once lived inside of me
Cornered my thoughts and turned you into a rumination,
I tried to find you.

But you were gone.
Really gone.
And there was a heavy stillness in my place.
On cold nights, I remembered the ferry and
All I could hear was the nun,
The nun who so many years ago told me:
"You will still be here
In the morning."

INVOLUNTARY PASSAGES

There is an open gate leading to a rocky path that
Takes me to an unseen place within a familiar space
Where thoughts play tricks within my own mind.

Over and over: I spin the kaleidoscope,
Mix the Technicolor cognitions and recycle
My ruminations… but return to a one-way street.

I go the familiar way and avoid the misleading turns,
But I always arrive at the same place with an opaque exit.
Some frown with disdain and say:
It just cannot be done.

What an anomaly; I gave up caring.
I wear the same blue striped dress on Saturdays
And eat indistinguishable apple pie on Wednesdays.
Why do I always hear the same steady beat of the rain
Assaulting the same tired fire escape?
I wear myself out.

Who designed and built this maze of convoluted
Complexities that drives my personal psyche?
Who made me his own practical joke in some
Attempt to always get the last laugh
As I age in this reflection of smoky cracked mirrors.

THE STATION AND THE BAR

Late last Monday night:
With one gasp, I was at the station.
Deep snow covered the ground everywhere
And covered me in whiffs of elixirs.

In that cold place
There was so much to see
As wet flakes fell on my eyelids
And blurred my vision in unwelcome ways.

But the little red train behind the station
Gave me reasons to stare.
So I stayed… and stared
At stuff I knew would melt into
Yesterday.

For no reason,
I wandered a different way and
I became lost and forgot to follow
A trail and go home to my home.

That was not my first missed connection.
There was a time decades ago when
I unfurled in full glory and
I stayed too long at Ray's Bar
In Estoril and missed the bus.

After a day at the sunny summer beach,
When it started to get dark and darker…
I left the fancy hotel towels
On the hot sand and I found that place
On the Av. Sabóia where I got
Drunk on Jack Daniel's and soda water
And talked to a guy who told me
I looked like Linda Darnell.
I fell in love with that handsome stranger

Because he knew his film noir
And the day was saturated into celluloid.
We left that place and of course there
Was a magical streetlight to help
Guide the way to any other place,
Any other place that would join
Other places in a reference place.

But I wanted to stay longer on that street.
I looked in a store window and saw pillows
That spoke of love and there were even ceramic
Angels to cherish during a drive with a stranger
Back to the city.

A stranger: an interlude, falling away behind me
When I returned to the city.

There are some places that stick inside me
And memories surface at the strangest times.

VINTAGE AIR

I traveled a long distance to reach
Canton, Ohio…

As a mountain of film history
Tailgated my thoughts and
Gnawed at me for miles, my mind remained
Inside my old Nova, the car my mother gave me
Because she needed a different vehicle
To fit all her hair rollers and Revlon's
Fire and Ice and her rosy rouges.

My mother always had to be the twin with the
Toni and she designed her look with great
Attention to mercurial defined detail
To appeal to the Canasta group or to
Attract other women and not my father.
That I know to be true.

I bent on Market Avenue N to show
Respect and to remember
Peggy Ann Garner
Who so long ago watched a tree grow
In Brooklyn and said
"Papa loved that tree."

I cried when she said that
Not knowing my backyard tree would one day
Be harshly cut down and my own green view
Would be destroyed so all I would see is some
Faded old ghost ad saying
"Sol Shapiro plumbing supplies."

These days, when a sign says "One Way"
I go the only way so on the corner
I inhaled the vintage air and took
Snapshots of the facade of the Palace Theater

With the fancy marquee.
Then later, when the sun went down in Canton,
I walked on tired feet with numb toes back to my new
Hotel whose light in the lobby was so bright
I squinted and tried to manage my dry eyes.

I went up to my room and hoped I could find the
Remote and perhaps with hands all bent and arthritic
Punch in the code at TCM On Demand which would
Send me back to the past, like
Marty McFly,
To a place where I could enjoy
"Junior Miss."

BORDENTOWN

This one goes way back,
Back to the morning the doll was unboxed
And the wrapping paper was so shiny
It reflected the bend in the day.

Decades ago, the doorbell rang...
Four eyebrows raised in arches, red lipstick
Covered many white teeth, and a kettle boiled.
The aunts welcomed them and celebrated the
Day they arrived on old Burlington Street.
That old storied house smelled like yesterday's mothballs
And in the dim light the teen sensed the ghosts of ancestors
Walking through the rooms of the house, a house that
Had many concealed rooms and probably
Many secrets to hide.

But they sat in the muted foyer decorated in bland colors
And had dark tea and sweet cakes and talked about family
And reminisced about distant relatives
Who at one place in time were so much closer
They could see each other's breath
Falling from tongues.

And then the teen climbed a very steep narrow staircase
To a room with a low ceiling and greeted an old uncle
Who lay in his bed covered by a white chenille worn
Bedspread and he beckoned for her to go closer
Because he did not even know her name.

That was not the first time the teen breathed air
On Burlington Street.
There was an echo from a day long ago
Of a time when the child was so young she had to hold
Her grandmother's hand when she left that house.
It was a hot summer day when all was still
And everybody walked more slowly.

The quiet sounds on the street soon melted away
As they moved closer to the corner.
They followed the sound of the happy music
Until they were in front of
The Clara Barton School.
The old one room schoolhouse was
Surrounded by a white picket fence.

Until that day parties were a different experience.
On that day it was red ribbons, red balloons
And red velvet cakes that stuck to her teeth
As would, in later years, her aunts' lipstick.

And inside everybody was playing and dancing
And doing little things that mattered.
They sat on a worn bench by the window and the view
Settled in and with one gasp the intoxicating
Memory of that party was forever set like
Solid stone inside her.

The hard rocks on the pavement during the walk back
Grew envious.

REVISITED

This one goes way back,
Back to the morning the doll was unboxed
And the wrapping paper was so shiny
It reflected the bend in the day.
And left nothing else to say.

Decades ago,
The doorbell rang and was answered by two dames
With four arched eyebrows and identical red lipstick
Smeared over two mouths with many white teeth.
Behind the cracks of the walls a kettle boiled
And the orange cat recoiled.

The aunts welcomed them and celebrated the
Day the cousins arrived on old Burlington Street.
That old storied house smelled like yesterday's mothballs
And in the dim light the teen sensed the ghosts of ancestors
Walking through the rooms of the house, a house that
Had many concealed rooms and probably
Many secrets to hide.
There were several rules there to abide. I digress.

They sat in the muted foyer decorated in bland colors
And had dark tea and sweet cakes and talked about family
And reminisced about distant relatives
Who at one place in time were so much closer
They could see each other's breath
Falling from tongues still wet
And many lyrical images were set.

And then the teen climbed a very steep narrow staircase
To a room with a low ceiling and greeted an old uncle
Who lay in his bed covered by a white chenille worn
Bedspread and he beckoned for her to go closer
Because he did not even know her name
But he knew the day was still the same.

That was not the first time the teen breathed air
On Burlington Street and sat in that foyer chair.
There was an echo from a day long ago
Of a time when the child was so young she had to hold
Her grandmother's hand when she left that house
And walk carefully not to trip over the yard's grey mouse.

It was a hot summer day when all was still
And everybody walked more slowly in a particular way
To define it was going to be a perfect day.

The quiet sounds on the street soon melted away
As they moved closer to the corner.
They followed the sound of the happy music
Until they were in front of
The Clara Barton School.
The old one room schoolhouse was
Surrounded by a white picket fence
To set the mood and create an almost past tense.

Until that day parties were a different experience.
On that day it was red ribbons, red balloons
And red velvet cakes that stuck to the child's teeth
Like an old woman's red lipstick so matte
It matched the shade of a Doris Day hat.
And inside everybody was playing and dancing
And doing little things that mattered or mattered not.

They sat on a worn bench by the window and the view
Settled in and with one gasp the intoxicating
Memory of that party was forever chiseled like
Solid stone inside her and perfume so sweet
Pooled around the floor in the heat.

The hard rocks on the pavement during the walk back
Grew envious and turned from yellow to green
And it looked like a movie scene.

The child grew to be a teen and is now old.
She stares into her frothy milk shake and cannot even
Find one last bit, not one flavor to savor as she sits and
Waits for her curtain to drop
And the janitor to enter and erase those days with his mop.

DIFFERENT DROPS

In the dark, a charientism:
The planned dry insult
Weepingly rude or falsely funny
Wicked or disparaging;
Dropped as the fly keeps flying
And settles in to share
The moment: a moment at the
Cinema in the Picture House
On High Street.

A soul departs, still in his seat
And nobody even notices.
That's how it goes and so he
Goes with grace to another place,
To wherever.

The comedy ends and the audience
Bends to gather their bags of stuff:
The candy wrappers that were tossed aside,
Crumbs of popcorn sticking to soles of shoes
And all expressions fall away.

Later, all cry for themselves
And their own inevitable ends.
And some laugh at the irony
While some express harsh disdain
And the bells ring at St. Mary's Church.

Much later, there was a different drop
At number 7:
A muted tired bingo club
Where everyone gathered for
A different thing, to forget everything
So nothing mattered until the drive home.
Eventually many widows drizzled away
And the view was transformed

Into a particular present.

Now, near to where the Picture House
Once stood on High Street…
In bright daylight, there's a "shop to let"
And an old red phone booth with a sign
Saying "coins and cards."
A somber man rides a scooter
On Beckett Road as he passes the launderette.

And in the cast of the
Afternoon shadows, a gongoozler
Stares at New Junction Canal, finishes
His salty lunch, pieces of bread fall to the water…
And he returns to his butcher shop
In Doncaster, to cut fresh meat.

BENDING TO ENTELECHY

The strong ship sails away from the
Harbor with one blast of a foghorn.
All other sad sounds do not fall away.
A dour mourner on land shops
For a headstone...
The marker that sets in graphics
And validates that another,
Who rolled and moved within
Contained flesh through many years,
Or maybe not many years,
Received a data wipe.

It's too morose, be quiet,
Do not talk of the inevitable
It's banter about tomorrow.
We do not whisper of such things
In naked terms, in ways that may show
We have no heart: live in the moment.
Let's grieve when the time comes;
But it will come.
It's not a moot point.

The bread has a shelf life
The contract has an expiration date
And the curtain eventually came down
In the Morosco Theater.

The tadpoles in the clear stream
Become frogs and jump through
Green grass and push around dirt...
And who will cry when they
Too fall by the wayside?

Who will weep for the fly
On the wall who only flies
In circles and looks for bits

Of food to eat?

As each day passes,
I mourn for the time I will
Lose my own consciousness.
Because when my end comes,
And it will come,
I will never get to read the final chapters
Of cousin Jennie's own book.
Will she on one warm day
Hike Mount Tam?

All the mountains of stuff I will never
See: all the sequels to films
Unfold as harsh losses.
There is no cure for this empty
Form of despair.

So I grieve all the time:
It's my particular brand of melancholy
And my personal bend to entelechy...
Because life can be as beautiful as a
Live memoir in an old silent movie
That never ends.

THE EMPTY PARK

You returned in the still quiet to
Dyker Beach Park and sat in the
Glare of broad daylight
Under the old night streetlight.

You lost parts of yourself as I did
When moments tumbled away
When so many of us went away.

That was the place where the
Chipped pieces of our button candy
Melted into washed swirls of abstract art…

Where yesterday's bumpy seesaw,
Broken now, points to a tired and
Rusty jungle gym where you chased me
As if catching me would be a brass ring.

The benches where the old grandmas sat
And gossiped about the cuckold
Are empty now and dirty snow has
Collected on the path where strollers
Stood at attention waiting to be pushed
All the way home.

You returned for seven days:
As if sitting *shiva* would
Give you sweet solace and comfort
And bring you closer to
Something that once was.

EYE PRINT MUSINGS

Pavel Tchelitchew, Hide-and-Seek:
The little girl in the red dress
Cannot see us… she hides
And we seek.

She of the basic brown hair
In front of the brown tree:
Legs askew, one arm bent
One arm horizontal
And around her a kaleidoscope
Of bright and muted colors
Define a masterpiece.

Sometimes eyes gaze on strong
Tinted reds or shades of oranges…
Layers of mellifluous paint in yellows
And greens and on closer inspection:
A keener chartreuse.

We watch and they watch and all wait
For the child in autumn and a
Diaphanous arm provides comfort.
Who among these witnesses is secretly
Prescient and prepared for this?
Then, the mother gives birth to one infant
Or maybe two: it's in the eye of the beholder.

It's the uncertainty of this piece
The vulnerability of this art
The indeterminate colors,
That gives viewers pause at MoMA.

Wikipedia describes the painting as
"Ambiguous imagery"
And I pause to think how far the years
Have pushed and changed the

Locations of interesting and pithy analysis.
Their interpretation instigates
Wild lucid dreams, because I can.

If Plato were to be reincarnated, he might
Create a new inspired philosophy about life
On faded parchment when he returned
To his thinking room.

Perhaps years from now, historical events
Will be bizarrely and objectively written
About by time travelers using fountain pens
On notebook paper and passed through
Wormholes where sociologists will sit in pods
And read with special eyewear the old news
And try to understand.

They will sit gobsmacked and confused by
Such a world that revolved around so much turmoil.
Their planet will have given birth to an environment
Where there is control over climate change and a
Peaceful and diverse form of Willoughby,
Designed long ago by Rod Serling.

With one turn, I move back to the present
And gaze at Hide-and-Seek.
The surprise in the children's faces
A bent arm, a strong foot
The arms, the feet
The hidden figures
So much swirling detail
Never give this work closure.

Just as all the viewers at MoMA
Have no closure…
Yet.

WHAT GROUNDS A TOWN

This town is painted with detailed brushstrokes
Within graphics that visually trickle by.

Drivers on the main street and
Passengers on the outskirts
Of these tangled streets
Forget what passed in the rear view mirror.

Later, maybe: the drivers and the passengers
Go to the drive-in to see comedies.

While at the same time,
Past times are always painfully
Remembered by victims and visitors
In the core, and they are not laughing.

Riders on trains pass stone walls where
On the other side black and white silent films
Once played on screens and now scraps
Of old newspapers from years
Gone by are reminders of layered agonies
That spill hopelessly to the lakes.

After one defined breath, walkers pause
In this town to stare at that place
And remain in place to share curious glimpses.

I myself stopped there one rainy night when deep
Melancholy drove me to drive, to drive in all ways
I could creep and through all paths my imagination
Could crawl, so I could think and make sense
Of the whole senseless.
And when I stopped on State Street
I inhaled and with one whiff
The total of all the layered misery
From all different harsh sides was inside me.

Strangers in other towns never knew of the
Solid prison next to railroad tracks where the mournful
Sounds of trains passing was a constant reminder
Of the past in which a life could have advanced
Along a different and less wrongful path
Leading to different ends.

Locals always whispered of inmates filled with
Despair who died inside that place and many still wait
For the ages inside that place so they too
Can die and reach the end of the line.

I thought of the lonely men who lived in solitary
Confinement and live in a bleak prison next
To railroad tracks where mournful sounds
Of trains passing filled and fill the air.
Hopeless inmates waited to die and still wait
For rightful justice to be served:
An *eye for an eye*,
Served up plain and simple.

Long after I left that place I heard for many
Nights, in my small city apartment and while alone
In own my bed, the sad faraway sounds of trains
Passing as they carried innocent riders to other places
And probably some measure of happiness…
In full blown living Technicolor.

On a rainy cold day,
I was disturbed when the wind blew
The curtains in and by the haunted and haunting
Sound of the blinds rattling.

WHEREVER HE WAS TAKING ME

I wanted to go.

In the air, the full bodied scent of musk and
Dried lavender presented as luminous illuminations
As my colorful dress fell in cascades around me…

I crept, in some trance, step by step down the
Narrow outdoor stairs of The Rialto Theater,
And as I staggered in almost old age to reach the
Bottom step, he was sitting there close to the sidewalk
As if he was waiting for me since forever.

He: a stranger I suppose, and he held
Nothing in his outstretched left hand except maybe
Something hopeful and different.
The light dimmed and the suggestion of something
Vague whispered as the mourning dove
Sang at dusk.

He wanted to take me to someplace strange and
Perhaps filled with bizarre hallucinations: so I could
Start again and feel the warmth of newness.
Yet, I sort of recognized the stranger as if he stepped out of
Some shadowy old film noir about some obscure prison and
I was seduced into his wicked life.

I was embraced by some fear but I wanted to walk him to his
Cell and remain there with him and stay there with him
Because his presence and reflection gave me strong comfort.

I knew this was not even real…
This was all make believe: like a
Child wishing for a
Black velvet party dress or a bride doll
Because she was brave enough to have
Her tonsils removed.

In woke moments, I knew this was confusing reverie
In a curtain call within the autumn of my years.

I was beckoned into celluloid by a charade,
By a practical joke, a mind trick and game
To tease me as I have always been taunted
With nonsense because I was always passing
Through life deciding who to be.

FISHNET STOCKINGS ON
A COLD WINTER DAY

On 45th Street on an overcast morning in winter:

I was a lofty vision with chipped ice up to
My ankles and adhesive bandages on the
Back of my feet…

My tootsies were all wrapped in blue suede
High heels which highlighted my shins covered in
Black torn fishnet stockings.

In the bitter air, from an open window
"Take Me As I Am" by The Duprees blared
As I hurried in the direction closer to the river.

Ruby red lipstick gathered and bled into
The soft wrinkles at the corners and under
My lips and I looked like I had eaten warm juicy
Cherry pie fresh from Bickford's oven.

My purple velvet beret sat on top of dark ringlets of
Curls that Toni owned and my brown wool coat was
Obviously the dinner for some hungry moths who lived
Sight unseen in my cramped closet.

But, on that cold morning I was going to work.
The blue Underwood was waiting for my fingers
Like my Aunt Ruth waited at the end of her day
For her dish of chocolate ice cream.

I was waiting and I waited.
I waited during many winters when ice would melt.
And I would wait for decades to be
Caressed by a lover who really cared.

TUMBLEWEED

Tumbleweed
Rolls with the wind.
And so he rolled along too.

He, who was so afraid of dying
And he has been dead for so long.

Back then, they still sold Chuckles
At the movies and after we left the
Balcony, we lived the stories that we
Watched on celluloid.

On a cool evening, we drove to the fair
And the mystic fortune teller
In the wooden box
Delivered a message that said we
Would sail together on the sea.

I was unsettled back then:
I lived with the illusion of romance
And I got drunk with the longing
When we were apart.

And now at night, with
One hand up and one hand down,
Through bare windows
I watch lovers in the alley
Making love and when the
Mourning dove settles in and the
Sun rises, I go to sleep.

CHALKBOARD

Through open windows
The colorless air hits the chalkboard
At the edges of the green.

The beef boils in the cafeteria
And the toys rustle in the sandbox.
The children chase between seesaws
And create tangles and visions of curls
While an old man passes on the sidewalk
And above, his wife hears his bones creak.

The teacher cleans the erasers
And ponders what to clean
And in the late afternoon
The sun lowers and bends
To bring closure to similarities
And to naked sameness.

Time passes and settles in
And creeps to a faded distance
Then crawls into dark bent night
As thicker air is created to
Nest within morning fog
As the dog barks in the lighted alley
Waiting to be fed.

And all that remains is the chalkboard
Washed clean at the end of every day
Waiting for something different
To be said.

DELINEATIONS

When you color in your scrapbooks
Do you stay between the rigid lines?
Do you remain constrained and not let
The nuances bend and bleed out?

The shades of all my colors bled out
Into blended running hot watercolors
The day the long series stopped.

Nobody else cried…
They all moved on into frenzied
Self-absorbed lives, but I got stuck
In the grey layers of my imagination.

I have always hated endings;
They are so final and so concrete
And there are no turns or going back.

So many stories are set in chiseled rock within
All the pathos and pain of the granite's past.
There is no way to change what drizzled down;
There is no way to undo past spoken words.

But before I fall asleep under crocheted perfumed
Elixirs, I write my own endings to episodes and
I change the paths within all the convoluted detours.

I can make the kiss last longer
I can undo a murder
I can bring back the dead
I can create open windows and unlock doors
I can reimagine different curled futures
For people who do not even exist.

And somehow that stabilizes me.

TRIPTYCH

In youth:
The shyness was the lid
Under which I covered my needs.
I was fluid in all ways
And it was only at night that
I could admit my truths.

In middle age:
I lived life within the null set…
I floated along in mundane ways
And just killed time
Rolling along in boring lanes
Doing the necessities.

It was only in old age:
That I would embrace unfamiliar desire.
The strong longing for passion,
Which festered unfulfilled
And fluttered like a dying moth,
Almost drove me to the brink
Of madness.

SHIPWRECKED

I remembered the silence within the
One turn… the turn at the corner that I
Believed would flatter my possibilities
And point me in a different direction.

But at the end of each day, I crossed the
Finish line at no particular extraordinary
Place: I was suspended in space where a
Past hardly mattered, where on new days
I bent to the bricks on roads that struggled
To keep me going.

All avenues had narrow lanes
With no wiggle room and allowed for
No deep different dives.

So I went this way, went that way
Many times knitting elixirs
In grey attics so I could
Navigate bridges
Drive through a tunnel
Take a train passing a river
Live in solitary confinement
Or get lost at sea and not feel abandoned.

When I reached the end, I finally
Understood nothing mattered:
Not my angers, not the songs I sang
Or my spoken words, or my written words
Scrawled like graffiti on the toilet wall.

It was only the distant sound of
A lover's heart still beating
That always should have
Brought me home.

THE WAY HE LOOKED AT HER

I have lived my entire life
Within my own head, consumed
With possibilities but never catching
That brass ring.

I went close to so many rocky borders
But never took chances
Or crossed any dangerous lines.

I danced with strangers at sock hops
And later passed through
Usual stages:
I dated this guy, went out with that guy,
Picked up guys at bars,
Wore boyfriend shirts,
And as the decades rolled by
I clung to unusual stages:
Developing crushes on men
Who did not even give me a side glance.

I rolled along this way or that way
And let time pass quickly under
No remarkable relationship umbrella.

It was just the way it was:
Some just fall through
The romance cracks.

But as I aged, my pages
Were showing sharper glimpses of
What eluded me.

The strong wind knocked something
Over and when I looked through the
Window and saw under a streetlight
The way he was looking at her,
I realized life had passed me by.

THE FLUID WALK

It was in the grey of winter that
Many things froze on the roads in a new town
The day I stopped at the red and noticed
The heavy blue wastebasket had tipped and
Fallen almost to the beckoning sidewalk.

All the chipped orange bricks under me soon
Softened and the dog barked from a
Low terrace letting me almost hear the air
Bend to his wants.

A teen crossed railroad tracks pushing his old
Grandmother who moved to the front as if
Smelling different whiffs would quicken
The familiar journey.

Backyards had gathered junk for sale…
But I saw under some tired rubble:
A photo of a smiling mother whose children
Probably lived far away.
I held families on daguerreotype and saw
Polaroids of babies pushed out yesterday who
Probably had babies they pushed out too.
All the babies in old age abandoned
These fuzzy photos… and so it goes.

A man pushed a stroller as if all he wanted
To be was a father and the theater
He passed, for a moment, captured his story.

On worn grass, frogs gathered at a park with
A wishing well and strangers watched strangers
While mountains in the distance
Blurred the horizon.

A diner advertised "pizza subs beer"
As if that was all that was needed at
The end of a day.

MANHATTAN BRIDGE THREE CENT LINE

So he was dead.
That was the news on a Wednesday
In January on Rivington Street.

When he died, her head did not
Turn this way or that way because
He belonged to another.
Her cheeks stayed dry.

She did not visit him
Until many years later
After he was in the ground and buried
And part of the *ashes and dust*.

But, one autumn day:
She took a trolley to Fulton Street
And then walked about four miles
To Green-Wood Cemetery.

She felt haunted by his remains
Under a crisp blue sky.
She put a rock on the headstone
And looked to the east
And imagined she heard
Mascagni's *Cavalleria Rusticana*
Which did make her finally weep
And she collected her sadnesses
So she would remember.

All the strangers that gathered
On the same day of that week
Walked carefully around the graves to not
Disturb the hush or the defined postures of
Those who were horizontal.
The many vertical who came to grieve
In selected ways separated
The living… from the dead.

SPILLED MILK

The past, defined by what was:
Green falling away to orange and
Becoming the white snow
That melts into a long series
Of endless reruns.

Maybe so, but time could be
Wrong and maybe everything just
Folds into itself in stacked layers
And all the colors blend into
A smeared fingerpainting
To mix it all up so we are always
Trying to get it right.

Yesterday, I crawled up five steps
And when I looked back
The path was deceptive.
There were no piles of important
Notes to beckon and show the way.

In old age, my lover's heart is beating
As he waits for me even though we
Have never met.

Bones are decaying in graves and
The heated conversation about last year's
Birthday menu now hardly matters.

I fall asleep in my bed with the windows
Wide open so I can wake to cold air.

All that is needed is strong coffee in
The morning and an old song on the
Victrola to help me remember:
To help me remember
What is about to happen.

ALONE IN THE STILL

The blizzard arrived and I prepared for the rerun.
It was always tough to awaken when there was
No morning sun, when the cold chill in the grey
Air through the open window shocked like sharp
Blue eyes just opened, shaped by sights of
Shady occurrences in last summer's shade.

The green grass next to the lace gazebo
Captured a passing lucidity in the pristine garden
As the petals of the red rose fell to transparency.

Another season passed after a lover's tongue
Glided over closed eyelids and disturbed dreams.
When he turned his head, I felt him disappear.

Oh! The aldehydic flattered him so.
I saw his scent, the scent that entered the room
Before he did and it burned my eyes.
He was that scent, the whiff of distraction within a
Middle chapter as he always struggled to reach
The soft pillow that waited for his return.

He passed through life gathering damaged parts
And repairing pieces of colorless stained glass.
I wanted out, he replied:
"Sorry to hear that, be well."

What seduces me now here… alone
Is the sound of the rain on the empty fire escape
Or the light that shines into my window at night
From the streetlamp below.

I limp into sameness and somehow that
Calms me.

PLACE KALEIDOSCOPE

One summer long ago, when my hair
Was still thick and long and dark,
I was living in Brooklyn again...

The light in the humid night would mix with the
Moonlight and shine on the bricks across the back alley
As silent Technicolor RKO pictures moved in naked
Cut-up images like a lucid slide show.
That brick wall had windows surrounded by
Green wooden old shutters, green broken shutters
That always reminded me in my solitude
That I was home.

One midnight, I saw or thought I saw, a shadow man playing
A violin on the other side of a window with green shutters.
A wicked lady with dark red lipstick sat on a pedestal
Behind the same window with green shutters.
She wore a red straw hat with red flowers and
A black silk kimono draped her rounded shoulders
While a blue time traveler with stained glass
Ribbons in her hair smoked a stale cigar.

In the dark, behind another window with green shutters
I saw an old lady wearing a black lace silk negligee.
She struggled to get up from a tired bed,
A bed with a stained velvet cover next to a lamp
With stained glass shades.
And there was an older lady in the same bed.
She of the faded black hair slowly turned
And revealed a tattoo on one buttock of a
Shadow man with a violin
And another tattoo on the other buttock of a
Wicked lady with red lipstick.

At noon, on one grey day when summer was almost over
I drove to Coney Island, a place that still had the sweet scent

Of lonely mystery and desperate pathos in the air.
I walked along the windy boardwalk and stopped
To sit on a bench, to sit on a wooden green bench
And watch the murky waveless ocean.

At 3 PM, a lady wearing red lipstick and a red straw hat
Sat down next to me and knocked on my forehead.
She tugged on my velvet sweater and with hot
Breath like expired rose perfume,
She whispered into my hollow ear.

After midnight on a faraway snowy night,
When I looked out of my window with green shutters,
There was no moon in the still night sky.

The memory of the violin player and the wicked lady
And the time traveler connected me to that sad still summer.
The sound of Bach's *Chaconne from Partita No. 2*
Cut through the silence and echoed in the old alley
As my stale cigar stained with red lipstick fell
From my wrinkled lips.

CODA

This life,

Lived like a dream through stained glass
In a hazy deciduous forest alone among strangers.
I am the most strange, I am the different outsider:
Feeling like a vacuous soul on an endless ride
On a forgotten Ferris wheel, high and low, low
And higher but waiting and left and dropped at the low.

The ride is always on endless bizarre looping roads
Upon which all unfamiliar sights become visible as
Mysterious grey sculptures in the rear view mirror.

My insides are weary from traveling through seasons like a
Naked Amnesiac: the past remembered and easily forgotten.

The ghosts of ancestors are speaking through dense fog,
Cutting through this bittersweet life through which I
Involuntarily passed without my written consent making
My passages all a crime, an extreme felony.

In time I sat perched all alone seeing possibilities but
Owning disappointments during touches by many who
Broke my damaged parts and stole my wail, my shouts
My distressed chiseled shadows and
My pale scratched echoes.

This life is now mostly all behind me pushing me to the
Now where I stand on a precipice not sure which way to go:
To the detour or the curve in the road or a stop sign or
Drive to the dead end or move miles away and live the
Same way in the same life: this red lighted life.

And as frightening as the journey has been during
The vivid Technicolor scenes and after midnights in film noir
In all the pain and anguish and panic…
All I really want, all for which I long
Is to stay longer, to remain, and not leave this place.

UNFINISHED WORK

In this concrete city when I wake up
And in the morning I hear the oddly
Placed song of the mourning dove,
I think about this:

It is sad I did not have a lifetime with him
But I am grateful I can have some time with him.

It is what it is,
And so it goes.

SIX POEMS

OLD THINGS

In this town,
There's an old round streetlight
And tied to that light is a droopy flag
And I thought it may have recently rained.
In front of a quaint antique shop,
Filled with Philco and Victrola radios,
A child on the sidewalk
Played Jacks.
And a mother, pushing a baby carriage,
Was wearing a blue poodle skirt
She may have bought at that
Dimly lit thrift shop on the corner.

IN THE PARK

In the town's park,
There is a gazebo where children
Can sit with their dolls
And eat cookies with sprinkles
That sit on fancy lace doilies and
Enjoy sweet iced tea
While their fathers
Sit on the bent grass and drink
Root Beers and talk of trivial
Things that later will matter.

PENTIMENTO

During another road trip,
While listening to
"Have You Heard"
By The Duprees, I came upon
This vintage place set in surreal
Graphics, which I found by total chance
While again searching for Willoughby.
This town is like an hallucinogenic pentimento
Revealing a museum piece finely decorated in
Soft watercolors: a place painted in blurred
Brushstrokes with an artist's keen attention
To fine detail and once discovered,
I wanted to stay
As if remaining there
Would endow me with a particular form
Of secret and strange breathless immortality.

DEFINED SPACES

There are two small green seats
In the park
That face each other
Separated by a cement sidewalk
So lovers have to stretch
To touch.

SENIORS

In the park,
There are four strong benches
All lined in a straight even row
So grandmothers can stare at wall art
Which in later years will become
Of great historical significance.
And that is rather fitting.
I imagine they must speak softly
Because even their breathless tones
Had to fit to keep this place frozen in time.

SLOWING DOWN

After that road trip,
I had to take the high road
And learn not to take myself
So seriously.
I saw how Willoughby is in
The eye of the beholder.
I cruised along and stopped preaching to
The choir and appreciated the small things:
A neighbor complimenting
My curly hair and
The mail on Saturday...
And even the sound
Of the heat coming up from the radiator
On a cold winter day.
What really matters
At any point in time
Are the personal passages and
The musical soundtrack
Within any stranger's memoir.

STREET POEMS

THIS PENTIMENTO

Via Comandante Simone Guli,
In Palermo, a street so old that
High above wives still hang the wash
Out over the black iron balcony gates
Next to green leaves and blue and white
Striped curtains falling out of windows.

Once children stood there with mothers,
Waiting for fathers to return home.
The red flowers now sit high over sad
Graffiti and a tobacco shop which
Serves as some reminder not
To obscure the view.

OPTICAL ILLUSION

On Edinburgh Street,
In Winnipeg, parts of the ground were still
Covered in snow under a crisp blue and
White sky that almost crackled with sharp
Definition and clarity.

It was there that I turned a corner
And stopped at a driveway and saw,
In the icy cold snow, carved footprints
That finally reached an almost
Tropically lighted home.

PICTURE PERFECT

On Tazewell Avenue Southeast,
In Roanoke, some houses sit very high
Above the street under a bleak grey sky.
The trees are suffering and bent and leafless
And the air appears to be chillingly cold.

I wonder who climbs those long steep
Staircases to sit closer to that foreboding
Sky, where clouds cling together trying hard
Not to let thin patches of blue peek through
Because the view might be less mysterious.

TO GET TO THIS PLACE

On Aleppo Road,
In New Freeport, there are wonderful
Things, rich and wonderful things.

Old houses made of dark crumbling
Wood that remembers what was,
A dry waterless sandy creek
And an old and tired bench
Where an old grandmother sat
And turned, with bent and gnarled
Fingers, the pages of a book
While whispering magical words
That filled a child's imagination.

Keep moving past a graveyard where
Old and broken and long forgotten cars
That yesterday were shiny new cars that
Once took children to faraway colorful fairs.

And past some jumping deer going up a
Steep hill to get back to the forest to hide,
To get back to familiar safe places.

A shiny white gazebo stands alone on
The grand grass where dolls sit
Wearing fancy hats and having sweet tea.

To get to this place you will need to
Go the other way, go that other way,
Go a different way to be taken away.

NOBODY HOME

Between Muirfield Road and Culduthel Road,
In Inverness, there is a street with no name.
But, you can get there.

An old stone building is quietly hidden
Surrounded by a low iron gate
In a lush green fragrant forest.
All sad sounds have fallen away
The many footprints are gone
And all that is left is the still.

The now boarded up windows
Allow no lights from inside to
Show the way home
And I think
Nobody is home
In this long ago forgotten home.

MELANCHOLY

On Second Avenue,
In New York City, I had dined on
Sweet baklava every week for years
Feeling this way... or that way.

On one cold January melancholy day,
Under threatening skies, I wore my balaclava.

And in the distance, I imagined or imagined not
That I heard Chopin's *Nocturne Op. 55 No. 1*.

DESERTED HOUSES

On McDonald Road,
In Lovington, on the dusty
Road under the blue sky
There is an old wooden
House that is deserted.
There's nothing left of the roof,
Or the porch, or the doors.

I traveled down that lonesome road
And saw another house, also deserted.
And then another, set far back and
Looking all broken and empty, too.

I suppose at some time people
Played here, and danced here
Maybe they even sang here
In these now empty rooms.

But, they are all gone now
And nothing is left to hear.
Not the songs they sang or
Even the sound of the wind
That once was, once was
Right there and heard
On days long gone.

WHERE THE ROAD STOPS

On Via Regina,
In Griante Como, I knew I
Was very far away from
My own home and
All places familiar,
All things remembered
And then easily forgotten.

This street with this view was
Created by some artist with sentimental
Sentiments and great attention to
Detail from his own mind's eye: the buildings
With arched entrances, the restaurants where
Diners eat outside under white umbrellas or
Under the clear blue sky next to the perfectly
Sweet green round trees near the boats
On the lake coming and going,
Going and coming.

The remote and fancy street looks out
Upon a gorgeous lake with mountains
High above in the distance on the other side
On all sides.

On the other side, there's a soft
Mist above those mountains with a
Tiny village sculpted right into the
Mountain above the view of the lake
Behind the red flowers, red flowers
On this side.

This place, where children grew up
And in later years returned to
The same place with the same view
Of the mountain under the mist
And the tiny village sculpted right

Into the mountain.

This might be a good place to stop
A fine place indeed, to stop.
Because after all, all journeys end
And where do I go from here?
Where can I go from here?

ACKNOWLEDGMENTS

WHAT WAY TO GO TODAY first appeared in 2009 at *The Daily Beat* blog, thanks to Rick Dale.

CODA first appeared in March 2021 in volume 2 of *Pinky Thinker Press*, thanks to Charly.

THE DISTANT LEFTOVER first appeared in April 2021 in *The Dillydoun Review*, thanks to Amy.

Thanks to Renée who provided the stimulus and the intermittent comic relief.

Thanks to "Sara" who was a patient great listener.

Thanks to Nicole Freezer Rubens for her gracious endorsement.

Thanks to Cheryl Benton for guiding me through the process and her kind words.

And thanks to Alice Quinn, former poetry editor of *The New Yorker*, who decades ago gave me hope when she complimented a poem and encouraged me to always feel free to try her with my work.

ABOUT THE POET

Photo credit: Frederick Piccarello.

Marjorie J. Levine wrote her first story, "The Long Wait," at the age of nine. She is greatly nostalgic and believes life's journey can be as beautiful as a memoir unfolding in an old silent movie. She is a standup comic, an actor, a blogger, an internet broadcaster, and poet. For thirty-five years she was an elementary school teacher. She lives alone in New York City.